How to Start a T-Shirt Business on Merch by Amazon

Jill b.

Table of Contents

Introduction

Before you read further, it's important for me to note that this is not a t-shirt design book. Rather, my aim for this book is to help to guide a beginner through starting a t-shirt business on Merch.

Many moons ago, my husband was a freelance t-shirt designer. Since then, we've played around with selling print-on-demand (POD) t-shirts using printers like CafePress.com. We featured our designs on our own website and, when there was an order, we would fulfil it and drop ship it to the customer. Sales were marginal.

Now, there is Merch by Amazon. According to an article in Entrepreneur.com, Google tops in searches, followed by YouTube. Coming up third is none other than Amazon. Amazon is the top search engine when it comes to shopping. Over 40% of product searches originate from Amazon.

What does that mean for you? It means that by taking advantage of Merch's platform, your POD merchandise gets to ride along the marketing powerhouse that is Amazon. Not only that, your products are fulfilled by Amazon as well. So, if the buyer has an Amazon Prime subscription, the POD order qualifies for free Prime shipping as well.

Merch by Amazon's Background

At the time of writing, Merch is quite new. The program that was initially developed for app designers to print T-shirts for sale on Amazon in order to promote their games. Merch rolled out in September 2015 but fortunately for non-app developers, Amazon opened the service to everyone. However, within weeks of Merch rolling out, t-shirt designers, especially those that already had large collections of designs, flooded the service.

Unable to cope with the demand, Amazon limited the service by making it available by invitation only. That is, you will need to request an invitation at https://merch.amazon.com/landing. I suggest set up a new and separate account Amazon for Merch, even if you have an account that you use for shopping. While you can use the same account to sell, I prefer to keep things separate.

When Merch sufficiently increases their fulfilment capacity, they will invite you to join. There, you will be placed in tier 1, which allows you to upload up to 25 T-shirt designs. When you sell 25 T-shirts, you will be upgraded to tier 2, which allows you to upload 100 designs and so forth. Higher tiers include 500 designs and a Pro level which is currently by invitation only.

The time it takes to get the invitation will depend on Amazon's capacity. You should receive an email to inform you of your acceptance but keep checking your account in case you miss the email, or in case the email arrives later than your acceptance.

If you've read some of my other home-business books like selling on eBay and self-publishing, I talk about needing to have as many products for sale as possible. The more products you have, the larger your digital footprint or digital "shelf-space" you take up. Think of your grocery store shelves that are filled with products by food giants like Tyson or P&G or Unilever. When you pick something up from the shelves, chances are that it is a product by one of these companies or a similarly large company.

While at this point, there is no way for you to have that vast number of products, you can adopt that idea and apply it to your business. More product on sale means that you have a higher likelihood that someone sees one of your products. Even if they don't buy that particular item, they may go on to buy something else from you. With Merch, since Amazon does all the storage, production and order fulfilment, your business can be scaled to as large as Amazon will allow. It is therefore to your benefit if you have as many T-shirts as possible for sale.

The question now is, if you're just starting out, how do you "tier up"? According to Merch, "to move up from the 25 tier, a content creator will need to sell at least 25 shirts from those they have created to move up to the 100 tier. Admission to these tiers are based not only on sales, but the quality of the products being sold by the content creator as well."

Some ideas to meet the quota to tier up would be to design some seasonally-appropriate shirts like Christmas or Valentine's Day. An alternative would be to approach organizations or nonprofits and offer to design something for them, which they can order in bulk either for promotional or fundraising purposes. If you don't already have a collection of designs, don't wait until you get that invitation before you start thinking about your designs.

Starting Out

Once you're invited, enter all your information including bank and tax information (so that you can get paid), as well as your business information. If you don't have a business set up, you can use your name as a sole proprietor.

Generally, it's a good idea to set up a business entity. In most states, you can register your business through your Secretary of State's website. Just Google, "[your state] Secretary of State". Registration fees vary but usually run upwards of $100. If you need to apply for a tax number or employer identification number (EIN), you can do so from the IRS website at http://hyperurl.co/ein. The entire process usually does not take more than an hour.

Note that this is not any kind of professional advice. I am not a legal, financial or tax professional so please seek the appropriate advice from a professional in your jurisdiction to discuss which course of action will best suit your situation and needs.

Find a Niche

If you're starting out, trying to figure out *what* to design can be paralyzing. Instead of trying to be everything to everyone and burning yourself out in the end, it's best to focus on a niche. By focusing on a niche, you can create a target audience or customer avatar.

This is in essence, a detailed profile for your target customer. The avatar will be in the form, "Jim is a single male in his twenties who is a high school or college graduate. He has a well-paying job and has disposable income. He likes to play video games, order take-out and hang out with friends in his free time."

Your customer avatar is *not* "someone who likes X". Knowing your customer avatar well will help you to figure out not only who they are but also where they live, how they live, what they buy, who they buy for etc. All this information will help you to figure out how to reach them with your products down the road. PickFu (http://pickfu.com) is one potential site where for a fee, you can poll a narrowed audience.

If you already have an existing business, brand or audience then you probably already have a niche following. Think about words, quotes, images or themes that can work with the audience that you already have. How about words that you like to say? Utilize the platform you already have. Ask your audience for input and ideas on what they might like to see in a t-shirt. You can use Survey Monkey (http://surveymonkey.com).

If you don't already have a niche, then you'll need to come up with one. You don't have to be interested in that niche to design t-shirts for it, but I think it certainly helps. Being part of that niche not only brings authenticity to your work, you'll already be familiar with your customer avatar (because you are that avatar either wholly or in part). If you're already into that niche, you'll also know the "inside" information -- the terms and lingo used within that niche.

To help narrow things down, write down your vocation, your job, your hobbies and interests, the foods or drinks you like, the places you like to visit, your religion, your favorite sports, the movies you like to watch and the songs you like to listen to. All these will help you to figure out the niche you want to target. You can even mix and match niches to come up with a sub-niche for a t-shirt idea.

For example, "Healthy-Living Mom" or "Zombie Gamer". Try to come up with ideas that you can scale up with little effort. For example, "Healthy-Living Mom" can be extrapolated to "Healthy-Living Dad", "Healthy-Living Goth Chick" and so on.

Keep your eyes and ears open. Idea prompts may come from any of these places:

1. Conversations (the things kids and teens say, in particular, can spawn ideas)
2. News
3. Movie and TV Shows
4. Sporting events
5. Trending issues popping up on social media (Snapchat/Facebook/Pinterest/Twitter etc)
6. Bumper stickers
7. Things you see at the mall
8. Articles in magazines
9. Other t-shirts

Ideally, the market you pick should be evergreen. For example, the dog-lover or cat-lover niche will be evergreen (if not, it stick around for a long time). Other markets may be seasonal (like Christmas or Valentine's Day). Niches like zombies or vampires on the other hand, tend to trend in and out of fashion.

Testing Your Niche

Google Trends

Once you've narrowed things down, how do you check the popularity of your chosen niche? I love zombie movies so I'm going to use zombies as an example. Google Trends (http://google.com/trends) is a great place to test the popularity of your niche. Here you can compare the trends over time or within specified regions such as within the US only.

The following graph shows how "zombies" have trended over time. I have also included "vampires" in a comparison graph (the vampire graph is the smaller, less popular graph). So, as you can see, zombies have trended up over the last 12 years but it is certainly off its peak.

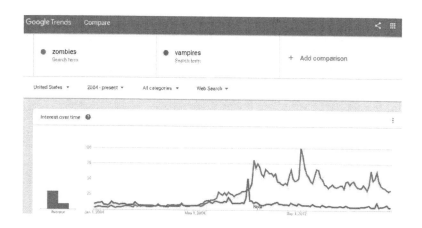

If you scroll down the page, there is also revealing information with respect to related queries and related topics which may help to spur more t-shirt ideas.

Facebook Ads Manager

You can also use Facebook to gauge your niche audience size. The layout featured may change over time but the idea should remain the same. Using your personal Facebook page, refer to the left menu that says "Create Ad".

Next, you'll be lead to the ad creation page.

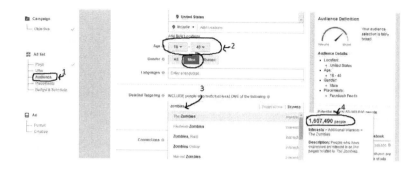

Click on "Audience" under the ad set on the left menu. From there, you can tweak your audience to get an idea of the size. At this time, for Merch research purposes, I would keep the audience location to the US, since that will be where your Merch customers will be coming from. Choose your age range and gender (that is where your customer avatar comes in). Then, type in your niche keyword.

Facebook will then pull up interests groups, which in themselves may give you some market insight.. Facebook will also provide the audience size in the right column. In the above example, we can see that our audience size for US men aged 18-40 is a little over 1.6 million. Not a bad number, but not huge either. Of course, Facebook is not the be or and end all when it comes to figuring out your market size but, it can help to give you some idea of whether your idea is viable or not.

Amazon Sales Rankings

Finally, you can do your research in Amazon itself. There are a few ways to conduct your product research on Amazon. The first and most straightforward, though tedious way, is by doing an alphabet search. To do an alphabet search, type in "t-shirt a", "t-shirt b" etc and go down the alphabet to see what Amazon pulls up.

Remember that Amazon is a shopping search engine so like Google, it will pull up popular search terms based on the letters or keywords that you type in. In the example below, you can see how Amazon completes my keyword search based on other popular searches. This is also a good trick to find keywords when you are adding terms to your listing description.

Once you've honed in on your search term, Amazon will pull up a list of relevant searches. Not all will be relevant for your research purposes because not all listings originate from Merch. Disregard items that are obviously not by Merch: non-T-shirts, shirt styles that Merch does not currently offer etc.

Easy ways to distinguish Merch shirts include the Prime icon, having a single price (rather than a price range) and having two images one of the shirt and the second showing three models, each wearing blue t-shirts posed next to corresponding size charts. If however, a design catches your eye, by all means look into it further.

Now that you've found a design that you think might be selling well, you can arbitrarily see how well it's actually selling on Amazon. Scroll down the product page to find the sales rank for that shirt. It should be under the product description.

Product Description

Product Dimensions: 15 x 12 x 1 inches
Shipping Weight: 4.8 ounces (View shipping rates and policies)
ASIN: ▮▮▮▮▮▮▮▮
Date first available at Amazon.com: September 1, 2015
Amazon Best Sellers Rank: #466,312 in Clothing (See Top 100 in Clothing)
Average Customer Review: Be the first to review this item
Would you like to give feedback on images?

Amazon ranks products in each category by a sales rank. The smaller the rank number, the better-selling that product is. So a #1 rank in Clothing means Amazon is selling *a lot* of that item. The rank is not representative of overall sales volume or total cumulative sales. Nobody but Amazon actually knows how the algorithm calculates sales ranks but it is based on sales compared to other products in that category. It is believed that historical sales contribute less to the ranking than more recent sales.

Since sales rank is relative to other items in that category, the product rank will not improve if all product listings in that category are selling more across the board. In fact, the item's sales rank may even worsen despite increased sales if other competing products are selling relatively more units.

In the example above, a sales rank of over 450,000 means not many of these shirts are selling. I recommending looking at Merch or similar shirts with a sales rank of below 10,000. Make sure you're also considering seasonal factors if the niche you are investigating is not evergreen. With this information, you have a better chance of designing shirts in a niche that has a built-in customer base on Amazon.

Be Social

Once you've honed in on your niche, it's time to be social with your target audience. Where you find them will depend on your niche. They could hang out in niche-specific forums, in Facebook groups, on Instagram, Pinterest, LinkedIn, Snapchat, Twitter, Reddit and yes, even MySpace.

Get a feel of the group, introduce yourself (in a non-spammy way) and jump into the conversation. Be genuine and helpful. Remember, it's not about "what's in it for me?", it's about "how can I help or contribute to the person/group?" In groups or communities where a majority adopts this outlook, everyone wins. I like to think of the adage, "a rising tide raises all boats" as being quite relevant.

As time goes on, you can ask for input, ideas or even design critiques from your group. If you're in an active and helpful group, some of the suggestions might even be telling and/or very helpful in focusing on your target. When your designs are ready, showing them off (in a non-spammy or pushy way) may even result in sales.

Designs

Again, this is not a book that will teach you how to design. Indeed, I'm not particularly artistic myself. That doesn't mean that I can't still design t-shirts with text and maybe some simple graphics. When it comes to text graphics, you will generally use two different fonts or interactions.

The fonts use generally include a bold sans serif font like Arial or Helvetica on top and a thinner (possibly script) font below. To quickly see your text in action in different fonts, use wordmark.it.

If you'd like to learn more about design, http://designschool.canva.com has quite a lot of good information not only on design but on branding, color theory, design trends and fonts. Other good places to get ideas from include Pinterest (http://pinterest.com) and other POD websites like Cafepress (http://cafepress.com), Zazzle (http://zazzle.com) and even Etsy (http://etsy.com) can offer inspiration.

You can also learn about t-shirt design, color palettes and typography (or font combinations) include Youtube, Google and the T-shirts on Amazon itself. Websites like Adobe Color CC (https://color.adobe.com/) or degraeve.com (http://www.degraeve.com/color-palette/) can even help pull out the color combinations of images that you upload.

This process can help you to isolate the color combinations of other designs that catch your eye. Don't limit yourself to t-shirt designs. Mugs and even pillow cases may just give you the inspiration you need!

Immature poets imitate; mature poets steal; bad poets deface what they take, and good poets make it into something better, or at least something different. The good poet welds his theft into a whole of feeling which is unique, utterly different than that from which it is torn.

-- TS Eliot

Pablo Picasso and later, Steve Jobs turned it into the quote, "Good artists copy, Great artists steal." By this, I am by no means advocating that you steal someone else's design. Rather, note the design elements, placement and font styles used. Learn and adapt what you see and put your own twist to it. *Make it yours.*

Copyrights & Trademarks

Please note that I am not a lawyer that the following information should not be construed as any kind of legal advice. This is merely basic information that I use to keep myself out of trouble when designing my tees.

Trademarks and copyright can be a maze, especially when it comes to grey areas like spoofs. Please consult an intellectual property lawyer before proceeding with anything that might be questionable.

When making your designs, make sure that you are not violating any copyrights or trademarks. These may include but are not limited to:

1. Company names (eg Pepsi, Nike, Disney etc)
2. Characters, mascots or their images (eg Mickey Mouse or Pokemon etc)
3. Sports teams and their logos and/or mascots (Red Sox, LA Lakers etc)
4. Schools, colleges and universities and their logos
5. Celebrity names and their likenesses (eg Elvis Presley, Michael Jackson etc)
6. Company slogans
7. Political figures, their likenesses and slogans
8. Movies & TV (eg Star Wars, Game of Thrones etc)
9. Comic Book characters (eg Peanut, Spider-Man etc)
10. Games as well as their logos, characters and images (eg Angry Birds, Gears of War etc)
11. Book characters (eg Harry Potter etc)
12. Certain non-profits (eg Breast Cancer Awareness etc)
13. Organizations (eg 4-H, Boy Scouts etc)

14. Government or government agency logos etc

Public domain images or characters are *generally* free for anyone to use. Note though, that different countries have different copyright terms before a work becomes public domain. In general, US copyright spans the life of the creator plus 70 years. In the US, according to 17 U.S.C. § 302, a work is copyrighted "95 years from publication or 120 years from creation whichever is shorter (anonymous works, pseudonymous works, or works made for hire, published since 1978)."

So, the works and characters of say, Shakespeare, are public domain. That however, does not mean that derivative works are public domain. On the other hand, although the original Snow White character in the Brothers Grimm falls under public domain, Disney Enterprises holds the trademark for the title in almost all forms.

While parodies *may* be allowed, it's an area that is contentious. If you are causing brand confusion, especially if your parody makes the brand or company look bad (which most parodies do), You might find yourself at the wrong end of a lawsuit. Personally, I don't think the stress and costs are worth the risk. However, if you want to go down this route, I strongly suggest seeking legal advice before proceeding.

Lesser known works may still be trademarked. You can search for trademarks for free at the US Patent and Trademark Office website (http://hyperurl.co/uspto). I normally search the exact word terms. I'm glad I did because my husband suggested that I call my t-shirt brand, "Off My Back". I thought it was brilliant but unfortunately, not original -- it was already trademarked by a T-shirt company. So, I abandoned that name.

Where Can You Find Images for Your Designs?

If you're not coming up with your own designs from scratch, where do you go from here? You can either use public domain images, or buy a commercial license to use an image. It is extremely important for you to be aware that just because something is online means that it's public domain.

So, if it's not in public domain, why is it on Wikipedia? Use on websites like Wikipedia is considered not for commercial use. In some cases, the creator of the image may allow use of their image as long as it's not for commercial purposes. Even images on US government websites are not 100% public domain. The rights to some of these are still held by the creator so make sure that you do your due diligence before using them.

With due diligence in mind, you might be able to find public domain photos or photos available for commercial use for free on Wikimedia Commons (http://hyperurl.co/wikicom). You can also try searching for photos on Flickr (http://flickr.com). Choose photos that are high enough in resolution. In general, the file size should be large -- around 1 MB in size or more. Otherwise, the resolution will probably be too low for use in print.

If you're using Flickr, search "The Commons", which can be found under the "Explore" button on the menu. Alternatively, you can search for photos by subject matter using the search box. You can then narrow down the searches by license (found in the submenu located under the main top menu). There, you may find some free photos that allow commercial use.

However, most commercial-use photos do not allow modification.

I personally like using Pixabay (http://pixabay.com). However, I also found a list compiled by Shopify that offer free photos for commercial use from the following websites:

1. Bucketlistly (http://photos.bucketlistly.com/)
2. Cupcake (http://cupcake.nilssonlee.se/)
3. Foodie's Feed (http://foodiesfeed.com/)
4. Getrefe (http://getrefe.tumblr.com/)
5. Gratisography (http://www.gratisography.com)
6. ISO Republic (http://isorepublic.com/)
7. Jay Mantri (http://jaymantri.com/)
8. Life of Pix (http://www.lifeofpix.com/)
9. MMT (http://mmt.li/)
10. Pexels (http://www.pexels.com)
11. Picography (http://picography.co/)
12. Raumrot (http://www.raumrot.com/)
13. Re:Splashed (http://www.resplashed.com/)
14. SplitShire (http://splitshire.com/)
15. Stok Pic (http://stokpic.com/)
16. Startup Stock Photos (http://startupstockphotos.com/)
17. Stock Snap (https://stocksnap.io/)
18. SuperFamous (http://superfamous.com/)

Use of some of these images may require proper attribution and/or they may not be allowed for use on merchandize. In my view, the attribution requirement makes its use on t-shirts or other merchandise difficult, if not impossible. Please read, understand and follow all the requirements of use before using an image.

Alternatively, you can also purchase images from places like Dreamstime (http://dreamstime.com), Shutterstock (http://shutterstock.com), Adobe Stock (https://stock.adobe.com/) or from a multitude of other stock image websites. Again, and I cannot stress this enough -- make sure that the images you purchase the license for includes allowing for use on POD products.

Some websites prohibit use of their images on POD merchandise. Others may charge more for POD use. Some may limit the POD run (for example, you may only be allowed to use the image imprint 1,000 times). In other cases, you may be required to modify the image *or* you may be prohibited from modifying it.

Note: Fonts may be copyrighted. There are websites like 1001fonts (http://1001fonts.com) or dafont (http://dafont.com), where you can buy fonts or download fonts for free for commercial use. Other fonts require payment prior to commercial use. Like photo and image licensing, some of the font licensing maybe confusing, with limits on the number of imprints you're allow to run etc. I like using https://fonts.google.com/ where I do not have to worry about licensing. The fonts are also free to use.

Creating Your Design

Once you have your graphics and/or fonts, you'll have to put it together. Merch suggests using Adobe Photoshop, Adobe Illustrator (http://adobe.com) or Gimp (http://gimp.com), which is free to use. Unless you have older versions of Adobe software, it is now only available on a subscription model. At the time of writing, it'll cost about $10/month with an annual contract to subscribe to Photoshop with Lightroom.

All the programs have a learning curve. If you're starting out, my suggestion would be to take advantage of Gimp since it's free. Photoshop has nice functions as well so if you think you might be able to make full use of the software, that might be the best option for you.

If you are a beginner, I don't really recommend trying to learn and use Illustrator because I feel that it is a more complex program and would probably be overkill for someone starting out. The subscription also costs more than Photoshop.

Keep Learning!

I understand that these software can be intimidating, especially in the beginning. But these days, you really have no excuse not to learn the basics. YouTube is a great way to learn the ropes. If YouTube doesn't turn up a suitable video, Google will pretty much take care of other questions.

If you prefer video tutorials, teaching platforms like Udemy (http://udemy.com) and Lynda (http://lynda.com) offer a range of courses that you can purchase. Udemy often offers discount coupons on daily discount sites like Groupon.com and LivingSocial.com. Some public libraries also offer free access to Lynda. Check your local library to see if this service is available in your area.

In a nutshell, important image editing functions to know, besides the basic line drawings, adding text and using erasers etc include:

1. Creating a new image with transparency (this is important especially for your t-shirt designs)
2. Image and text resizing/transformation
3. Canvas sizing or resizing
4. Wand selection (which allows you to select certain colors in the entire image and either change or delete it)
5. Using layers (it's a good idea to add each new element in a new layer for easier manipulation later)
6. Text manipulation
7. How to upload new fonts
8. Using filters

The Minimal Viable Product

The first version of Gmail was literally written in a day.
– Paul Buchheit, creator and lead developer of Gmail

Once you get the hang of the software, you can start testing your design ideas on the market. If you view this business as a startup (that is, a startup that doesn't have financial backing), then you can start creating your minimal viable products (MVPs).

In the startup world, a MVP is when as little as possible resources are invested into a product before it is released to the market. Once released, you can then continue testing ideas, color combinations, font use and various other iterations of your idea. Keep refining the product until it seems to hit the market. If it doesn't work, you didn't invest so much into it that you can't afford to abandon the design.

Hiring Designers

I won't go this route as a startup but if you have some money to invest and don't want to deal with coming up with your own designs, hiring a designer is an option. These days, the options where you can find a designer is mind-boggling.

to find designers include 99Designs (http://99designs.com), Fiverr (http://fiverr.com), T-shirt Factory (http://www.tshirt-factory.com/), freelancer (http://freelancer.com) and Upwork (http://upwork.com). If you want to deal with a local designer, you can even post a want-ad on Craigslist (http://craigslist.org).

You have to be careful when hiring designers especially if they offer lower-end price range designs. Firstly, you have to make sure that they didn't rip someone else's design off. Unfortunately, this is not always easy to ensure. The risk, I think, is even greater if you hire a designer who lives in a country that doesn't have strong intellectual property laws.

Ask to see their portfolio of designs. You'll not only be able to get a feel of their style and work quality but you'll also be able to see if they possibly ripped something off. You can upload images onto TinEye (http://tineye.com) or Google Images (https://images.google.com) and do a reverse search on the images. Also be wary of portfolios that include copyrighted or trademarked images unless they did the design for the rights holder. *That is, do your homework!*

Remember that it will be *you*, not the designer who will probably ultimately be responsible for any infringement claims that arise. Also, chances are that you'll have a tough time trying to file a claim against your designer, especially if they live in another country.

When you're buying the design, make sure you're buying full commercial rights that will allow you to reproduce that design on T-shirts (or possibly even other merchandise down the road). You will also need to consider if you want to purchase exclusive, worldwide commercial rights or not. This option usually costs the most.

Exclusive commercial rights means that the designer does not have the right to resell the design to someone else, or to reuse it. Some rights may be regional, meaning you can only sell the design in certain countries or regions. Some rights or licences may limit you to the number of imprints (meaning you can only produce for example 10,000 pieces of merchandise featuring that design).

In other cases, you may have "first rights", meaning you get to use the design first and, after a specified period of time, the designer can resell the design to someone else or reuse it. Some licenses may allow you to modify and build upon the original design and others may not.

There may be other rights that I am not aware of and/or didn't cover here. Personally, I won't buy any designs where unlimited exclusive commercial rights are not granted. Again, I am not a lawyer so if you're planning on buying designs, make sure you know what you're buying and consult an intellectual property lawyer if you have any doubts.

Designer's Use of Images/Fonts

Many designers will keep their own collection of images and/or fonts for their designs. Bear in mind that although they may have purchased the license to use the images and/or fonts commercially, that does not mean that you have the right to use said intellectual property for your POD merchandise.

That is, commercial licenses are almost never transferrable. You cannot use the design elements that your designer bought for use on your merchandise. Instead, you will need to buy the rights to use the images/fonts *then* have the designer put the elements together for you. Communication with your designer is key when dealing with hired design help.

If you're on a budget but need to enlist the help of a designer, a lower-priced designer may be your answer. They may just be the person who can help put together or tweak your elements, typography, placement or color combinations so that the final product is better than what you've been able to come up with.

Copyrights

Copyright laws vary from country to country. Since Merch by Amazon is based in the US, you will at the minimum, have to adhere to US copyright laws. Again, I am not a lawyer so please consult one if you need actual legal advice.

In the US, copyright law does not protect an idea in itself. Instead, it protects the expression of an idea. So for example, the theory of something is not copyrightable but writing, drawing or recording of that theory is. The nuances can be difficult to differentiate so you might want to clarify any potentially expensive infringement questions with a lawyer.

As long as your work meets basic copyright requirements, your work is copyrighted as soon as it is created. You do not have to include copyright notices but the lack of notices may reduce damages in an infringement lawsuit. Registration is not required to grant copyright. However, registration is required before a lawsuit can be filed.

You can register your work online with the US Copyright Office at http://www.copyright.gov. Application fees start from $35. Registration not only backs you up in a lawsuit but also helps the Library of Congress to build its collection of works. Once you've figured that you've hit some winning design ideas with your MVP, it might be worth your while to register your design.

Listing Your T-Shirt

The Merch dashboard is pretty straightforward. When designing your shirt, make sure that your canvas is set to 4500 x 5400 pixels (15x18 inches) at 300 dpi with a transparent background. You can download a t-shirt template from Merch but in my view, it's not really worth the hassle downloading. Just set up a canvas in your software with the dimensions that I described above.

All design files should be saved in PNG (.png) format. In most cases, the design should be centered and fill almost all the space. However, some designs may do better if it's shifted a little higher or lower on the t-shirt. Regardless, your final image size must be 15x18 inches at 300 dpi, even if some of that space is not utilized.

T-Shirt Fit

You can add designs to both the back and/or front of the t-shirt. However, if you upload designs on both sides of the shirt, your base cost price will increase by a few dollars. Next, you have the choice of printing on 100% cotton Anvil classic, regular fit shirts, or on 100% cotton American Apparel slim fit shirts.

The difference in the shirts is in their fit but American Apparel shirts also have a slightly higher base price. You'll therefore need to charge a slightly higher price to get the same royalty payout as if you used Anvil. If you're unsure as to what fit your audience prefers, you can do two separate listings for each individual design, one using Anvil and the other using American

Apparel. Time and sales will reveal which fit your audience prefers.

Sizing & Colors

All shirt listings have three sizing options: men, women and youth. I recommend including all size options, regardless of your target audience because larger women or youth for example, may buy a men's sized shirt while smaller women may buy a youth-sized shirt.

With regard to t-shirt colors, at the time of writing, Amazon offers a choice of 15 colors. However, you can only choose up to 5 colors per design. Merch recommends using no more than 3 colors per design but I don't see any reason why you shouldn't use all the 5 color options.

So what colors should you offer? I couldn't find any actual statistics on color popularity but from my research and information from long-time T-shirt screen printers, the basics: black and white are the two biggest selling colors in the US. The grays follow in a distant second. So these would include grey and asphalt. Lower on the list include reds and blues.

The problem is that a design normally works either on a dark background or a light one. One way around this problem will be to design two variations to your design (in two separate listings) -- a light version that looks good on a dark t-shirt and a dark version that looks good on a light t-shirt.

Offer the main popular t-shirt colors but don't discount colors that you personally won't normally wear. For example, I look terrible in yellow and green but I have friends who look good in those colors. Spread your color options out so that you can get a feel of what your *audience* wants to buy.

Of course, your t-shirt color choices should not clash with your design's color palette. Colors like maroon on red or green on green for example, generally do not work well. You can also vary your design and color to target the different genders. I tweak some of my designs to target either men or women and choose a more pastel palette for the latter and a darker palette for the former. Women also buy darker colored shirts and vice versa so offering an another variant will be a good idea.

Again, you can use websites like Adobe Color CC (https://color.adobe.com/) to test out color combinations. In most cases, if the image "fades" or blends into the background color, the design won't work to its full potential. Try another t-shirt color.

Pricing

Merch pays t-shirt vendors a royalty for each sale based on the selling price - base price. The base price is set by Amazon. At the time of writing, Merch's base price is a little under $13 for a single-sided Anvil shirt and about $1 more for a single-sided American Apparel shirt. Your royalty payout is any amount over the base price that you set.

Merch allows vendors to price their t-shirts up to $49.99 but trying to sell a $50 t-shirt will be tough. You ideally want to price your t-shirts as high as the largest segment of your audience will bear. If you are a bargain shopper, do not project your low price points on your t-shirts. Remember that there is a reason why both Kia and Porsche exist: they cater to different markets.

Generally, text shirts, especially if they are plain, sell for less than shirts with intricate graphics or unusual designs (see the earlier chapter on coming up with your own twist on things). Most t-shirts sell in the $15.99-$19.99 price range. However, research shows that people equate a higher price to higher quality. If you have something different, cool or unique don't be afraid to price higher. If you have something less original, then expect buyers to shop around and possibly buy from the cheapest source

Don't be afraid to test price points. If you're working with a MVP, you're working with quite a bit of flexibility. If the design is selling well at a price, try inching your price up a little. If sales drop, are you still making more or less overall? Watching your bottom line, rather than the price of the individual shirt should be your main objective.

If you're selling a lot of shirts at a cheaper price, you might be making more money overall than if you were to raise your price and sell fewer. Nothing is set in stone and you won't know unless you tweak different aspects of your listing.

Listing Description

Merch doesn't give you a lot of leeway when it comes to the listing description. But there are a few sections that you can customize: brand, title, bullet points and description. Try to optimize these sections to help your listings show up in searches. Since about 40% of product searches originate from Amazon, you want to try to make sure that buyers looking for your product *see* your product.

Brand

The brand is searchable within Amazon's search engine so it's a good idea to use a keyword-rich "brand name". For example, you can enter the brand as "zombie t-shirt" or "funny zombie t-shirt". Include your niche term + a descriptive keyword + the word t-shirt or tee or shirt in your brand section.

Do not leave out the term "t-shirt" or a variant of it because you want your shirt to appear to anyone who is looking for t-shirts. You may even want to put all three keywords: t-shirt, tee, shirt into the brand section to cover all your bases.

An advantage of branding all your shirts in the same niche with the same keywords is that Amazon will automatically include a clickable link on your brand name, allowing buyers to quickly see the rest of your designs. The downside however, is that copycats can do the same and easily find all your designs with a click of the mouse and copy all the designs. I'll discuss the issue of copycats in the next chapter.

The "brand" doesn't have to to be the actual brand name of your t-shirt. If you want to include your t-shirt brand name as well, my suggestion would be to add something like "by [insert your brand name]". So, your brand description would look something like, "funny zombie t-shirt by [insert your brand name].

While you don't have to include a brand name if you don't have one, I recommend doing so. This way, your buyers can at least search for your brand name to pull up all your designs. Copycats can do the same but it requires a little more than a click of the mouse to find all your listings. You don't have to build a brand but I encourage you to do so. As I quickly found out, the brand name that you came up with may not be so original. Just make sure that your brand is not a brand that's already trademarked.

Title

Besides the brand, the title is also searchable by Amazon's search engine. This is a crucial section that you should fill with keyword-rich text. This would be a good place to put in your t-shirt's caption or text. For example, "I'm a zombie gamer men's male adult t-shirt". Here, you not only included the caption/text but also included the niche/target audience, the size and the gender.

If you're at a loss for keywords, use the keyword search idea in Amazon's search box as I described earlier. You can use MerchantWords (http://merchantwords.com) to test keywords. MerchantWords is a paid subscription service (at $30/month, it is not cheap) but you can search up to 5 keywords a day for free. The site will then pull up the main keyword searches on Amazon US, as well as the categories that these words are most searched in. There are more functions that come with the paid subscription but if you're just starting out, I suggest just going with the free version.

Try to add as many relevant keywords to your title. Note that I said *relevant*. It will not look good if your listing looks spammy because it's keyword-stuffed. Ideally, the title should read normally but try to use the entire number of characters allowed in the title to maximize your searchability.

Bullet Points

Although Amazon includes some of the bullet point information automatically, you have the option of adding two more bullet points within the description. The bullet point information is searchable on Amazon so try to include as much keyword-rich relevant information as possible.

Including information like t-shirt colors available and applicable seasonal references like Christmas, Mother's Day (for something mom-themed) or Valentine's Day can help boost your shirt's visibility if someone is searching with those terms. Don't neglect to include other more generic terms like "funny", "quotes" or "quotable", "unisex" and "novelty" in this section as well.

Description

Although Amazon's search engine does not scan the text in the description area, it is still a good idea to fill this area with keyword-rich information as well. The reason is that Google's spiders will still crawl Amazon's description area. Since Amazon already ranks highly on Google, having Google scan your description is a great way to drive customers from another platform to your listing.

The Review Process

Once you're done with the listing, you're ready to have your design printed. At this point, you have the choice of either saving the listing, if you're not ready to submit the product yet; or you can send the design through Merch's approval process before the listing goes live. The approval process normally takes a few hours.

At this point, you can choose to make your t-shirt public after the approval process, meaning your shirt will appear in Amazon's listings and will be available for sale to the public. You can also choose to make the link private, which will allow you to buy a sample t-shirt to check the print before you approve the shirt for public sale.

It would be a good idea to order a sample t-shirt to get a feel of the tee before making the listing live, especially in the starting stages of your business.

The private listing option is also useful if you're offering custom designs for private sales to organizations. All you need to do is to provide your buyer with that link and Amazon will take care of all the order fulfilment logistics.

Copycats

Unfortunately, even though I've advocated taking the high road and coming up with your own designs, others may not be as scrupulous. In fact, some t-shirt sellers may not even have any original designs at all, stealing everything from others.

Thieves can steal your work in a variety of ways. They might steal your entire design, your description, your brand and/or a combination of these elements. They may use Merch to sell the stolen designs, or they may be third party sellers using Fulfilment by Amazon (aka FBA, another selling platform that does not include POD services). With FBA, the seller would have produced the copied t-shirts without Amazon's POD service.

In other cases, the t-shirt company may rip your design and sell it on other POD platforms, on eBay or possibly even on their own site. If you see an infringing item on Amazon, you can report it online at http://hyperurl.co/amazonreport or if you prefer to submit a report in writing, send the following information to the address below:

1. An electronic or physical signature of the person authorized to act on behalf of the owner of the copyright interest;
2. A description of the copyrighted work that you claim has been infringed upon;
3. A description of where the material you claim is infringing is located on the site;
4. Your address, telephone number, and e-mail address;

5. A statement by you that you have a good-faith belief that the disputed use is not authorized by the copyright owner, its agent, or the law;
6. A statement by you, made under penalty of perjury, that the above information in your notice is accurate and that you are the copyright owner or authorized to act on the copyright owner's behalf.

Copyright Agent:
Amazon.com Legal Department
P.O. Box 81226
Seattle, WA 98108
Phone: (206) 266-4064
Fax: (206) 266-7010
E-mail: copyright@amazon.com

Courier address:
Copyright Agent
Amazon.com Legal Department
410 Terry Avenue North
Seattle, WA 98109-5210
USA

Other selling platforms should also have their own section where you can report infringing items to. If an infringing item is listed on someone's website (not a selling platform), you may have little recourse other than to send them a cease and desist letter, which they may or may not abide by.

Amazon and other websites are aware of the problem. However, it may take a while for them to take action against the perpetrator. It is often an issue where you're playing Whack-A-Mole. Get rid of one vendor and another one, or maybe even the same one, might pop up somewhere else, usually under a different name.

Don't let this problem cause you too much stress. Even the big boys like Disney cannot stop imitators. Report what you see and give yourself a little pat on the back knowing that you're putting out stuff that's good enough to be worth copying. Keep producing designs and be the trailblazer.

Trademarking Your Work

If you feel the need to keep ahead of copycats and if you've hit an evergreen niche that is bringing in a decent income, you may want to consider trademarking your design. This is a more expensive route than merely registering your copyright. Explanation of the nuances of trademarking are best left to a legal professional. However, some things like text might be easier to protect with a trademark rather can a copyright.

Trademarks cost more to register -- they start at $225 as compared to starting at $35 to register a copyright. The trademarking process is fairly straightforward and can be completed online at https://www.uspto.gov/trademark. The USPTO requires you to do a trademark search to ensure that what you're trying to trademark does not infringe on something that has already be trademarked.

The USPTO however, recommends that you hire a legal professional to help with the process. Once trademarked, be prepared to defend your intellectual property and with that comes potentially high legal fees. Consider your pros and cons before proceeding with this option.

Marketing

Once you have your designs, in most cases, your t-shirts will not be the case of "if you build it, they will come." If it is, kudos to you! You've hit an underserved market. However, chances are, you'll need to market your products. The topic of marketing can fill libraries. However, we can in a nutshell, break it up into online and offline marketing. Here are some ideas to consider implementing:

Offline Marketing

A simple offline marketing tactic would be to give your t-shirts away. Give them away to friends and family. Wear them yourself. I print custom shirts with text on the back saying, "Like this shirt? Order yours today at [my website]." I also have a small version of the t-shirt design underneath the text. Wear your shirt to a places or functions that you know will be attended by your target audience. You never know who might like it enough to visit your site and buy it!

Online Marketing

There is a gamut of online marketing tactics ranging from paying for ads on Amazon, Google, Facebook and other social media outlets, to free marketing tactics (without being spammy) like posting on websites like Reddit and in forums where your target audience might visit.

As I mentioned in earlier chapters, free online marketing tactics can include posting your products on forums where you've been sincerely active on (and not spammy), as long as it's allowed by the site host. Pitch relevant topics to relevant podcasts or offer to guest post on blogs. The goal is to offer their audience value, not spam their platform. Some hosts may require a sponsorship fee or may have submission guidelines so make sure to follow them.

If you're looking to be a guest on podcasts, PodcastGuests.com is a good place to keep an eye out for queries. The site sends out emails every Monday with a list of shows looking for guests.

If you're trying to get media coverage, Help A Reporter Out (https://www.helpareporter.com/) is a good place to pitch to daily reporter queries. The service is free as long as you don't register to as an expert source. Media outlets will vary and many queries are time-sensitive so you have to be ready with your pitch. Most of the smaller outlets (and even some big ones) will however, reward you with a link back to your website if your pitch is accepted.

Pin and post images of your tees on Pinterest and Instagram. If you're active on other social media like Facebook or Twitter, add images of your t-shirt as well as your website information to the cover of your personal page. Be active and contribute to groups. If people like what you say, they may check out your main page and see your products.

Paid marketing tactics include pay-per-click ads on Google, Amazon, Facebook, Twitter and even Pinterest. Depending on your target audience, one site may give you better returns than another. For example, if your audience consists primarily of women, you may fare better advertising on Pinterest. In general though, Facebook advertising might be the best way to go because you can target very specific audiences. It is a tweaking process and can become a time and money suck so try different things but allocate your resources accordingly.

Setting Up Your Website or Domain Forwarding

Having your own website isn't 100% necessary but it is a good idea to have. The reason being that when you are marketing your t-shirts, you want to drive traffic through a website that *you* control. I say this is because as great as Amazon is as a selling platform, you are a digital sharecropper.

That means that you are at the mercy of Amazon. They may change their algorithms, reduce visibility or in extreme cases, suspend your selling account. Who knows, maybe five to ten years from now, another disrupting company or technological advance may come along and overshadow Amazon.

If you're marketing and building your business, you might as well drive customers to your site and build your brand instead of sending buyers directly to Amazon. Additionally, if you drive customers to your branded site before sending them on to Amazon, Amazon will pay you 4-6% in affiliate sales commission.

That not only includes a commission on the sales you make on your shirts, but also on just about anything else your customers buys within 24 hours of clicking through your link. You will still get your commission even if the buyer closes and reopens Amazon for a later purchase, as long as he/she doesn't click someone else's affiliate link before making their purchase.

Sign up to be an affiliate at https://affiliate-program.amazon.com. Signing up for Amazon's affiliate program entails a lot of terms and conditions so make sure that you read and understand it before using the links. Failure to comply with their terms may result in termination of your affiliate account and/or your earnings.

These days, there are many places to set up a website and to register a domain name. Many web hosts offer free domain registration with purchase but it is a good idea to register your domain separately with a different registrar. That way, if you lose the web host or want to transfer to a different host for any reason, you still have control of your domain name.

I use Namesilo.com. At $7.99/year with no annual increases, it is the cheapest domain registrar I've found. Other registrars include GoDaddy.com and NameCheap.com. With regards to web hosting, your options also run the gamut, ranging from your own hosting to using Wordpress.org to hosts that include pre-designed web templates like SquareSpace.com, Wix.com or Weebly.com; to storefront websites like Shopify.com, WooCommerce.com, BigCommerce.com and BigCartel.com.

If you are not interested in setting up your own website, you can subscribe to a domain forwarding service like GeniusLink (https://www.geni.us/), which will allow you to not only use your own domain name but have the forwarder add your affiliate link during the forward. So, when the customer types in your website URL, they will automatically be forwarded to Amazon's page but you will also earn your affiliate commission when the buyer is sent to Amazon and places the order.

Diversifying

"Amazon fortunes come and go, but when you put systems in place to cultivate an audience on other vendors, you have a steadiness of earnings to use as a baseline. I personally keep my business operating expenses 50% or less of my other than Amazon vendors just in case I ever lose Amazon." -- Elizabeth A. West, indie author

Ms. West is wise. While her quote refers to not confining self-published book sales to just Amazon, the same can be applied to your POD shirts. Once you have your t-shirt design up and running, you might want to start diversifying your marketplaces. I believe that Merch will in time, adhere to the 80/20 Rule. That is, 80% of your sales come from 20% of your efforts. In this case, listing your designs on Merch will likely result in 80% of your sales versus listing on other sites.

That said, you never really know where your 80% will come from until you test the other storefronts as well because each has its own audience, buyers and followers. Many, but not everyone shops on Amazon. Merch does not demand design exclusivity so why not upload them onto other POD sites as well?

POD websites include: Cafepress.com, Zazzle.com, SpreadShirt.com, RedBubble.com and Society6.com. Other POD services like Printful (http://theprintful.com) also offer plugins where you can sync your shirts to a select number of storefronts including Shopify.com, GumRoad.com and WooCommerce.com. If you add a Shipsaver.com subscription, you can even have them process Etsy orders for you.

Conclusion

As with any business, there are no guarantees that you will make a lot of money. Buy hey, there are no real guarantees in life anyway, except death. For me, Merch is a way to add to my brand while generating another income stream and diversification without needing me to invest resources towards the fulfilment process.

If you're looking to study the t-shirt business further, I recommend these other two books, "Threadless: Ten Years of T-shirts from the World's Most Inspiring Online Design Community" by Jake Nickell, "Thread's Not Dead: The Designer's Guide to the Apparel Industry" by Jeff Finley and "Launch a Kick-Ass T-Shirt Brand" by T-Shirt Magazine.

Sign up for my newsletter at http://byjillb.com and get THREE e-books for free:

HOW TO KEEP BACKYARD CHICKENS
CAN DOS & DON'TS
THE MODERN AMERICAN FRUGAL HOUSEWIFE

Disclaimer and Disclosure

This guide is for entertainment and informational purposes only. The author and anyone associated with this book shall not be held liable for damages incurred through the use of information provided herein. Content included on this book is not intended to be, nor does it constitute, the giving of medical or professional advice. The author and others associated with this book make no representation as to the accuracy, completeness or validity of any information in this book.

While every caution has been taken to provide the most accurate information, please use your own discretion before making any decisions based solely on the content herein. The author and others associated with this book are not liable for any errors or omissions nor will they provide any form of compensation if you suffer an inconvenience, loss or damages of any kind because of, or by making use of, the information contained herein. Any opinion given is the author's own, based on her experience. If in doubt, always seek the advice of a professional who can advise you appropriately before acting on any part of this book.

This book contains references and links to other Third Party products and services. Some of these references have been included for the convenience of the readers and to make the book more complete. They should not be construed as endorsements from, or of, any of these Third Parties or their products or services. These links and references may contain products and opinions expressed by their respective owners. The author does not assume liability or responsibility for any Third Party material or opinions. The author is the owner of Chicken Armor hen saddles and profits from sales at chickenarmor.com.

Resources

Merch by Amazon (http://merch.amazon.com)

EIN Registration http://hyperurl.co/ein
US Copyright Office at http://www.copyright.gov
US Patent and Trademark Office website (http://hyperurl.co/uspto)

Free & Paid Classes
Coursera (http://coursera.org)
Futurelearn (https://www.futurelearn.com)
Lynda (http://lynda.com)
Udemy (http://udemy.com)

Researching Niches
Google Trends (http://google.com/trends)
PickFu (http://pickfu.com)
Survey Monkey (http://surveymonkey.com)

Design Inspiration
Cafepress (http://cafepress.com)
Canva Design School (http://designschool.canva.com)
Etsy (http://etsy.com)
Pinterest (http://pinterest.com)
Word Font Samples (http://wordmark.it)
Zazzle (http://zazzle.com)

Color Palettes
Adobe Color CC (https://color.adobe.com/)
Degraeve.com (http://www.degraeve.com/color-palette/)

Images
Bucketlistly (http://photos.bucketlistly.com/)
Cupcake (http://cupcake.nilssonlee.se/)
Flickr Commons (http://flickr.com)
Foodie's Feed (http://foodiesfeed.com/)
Getrefe (http://getrefe.tumblr.com/)
Gratisography (http://www.gratisography.com)
ISO Republic (http://isorepublic.com/)
Jay Mantri (http://jaymantri.com/)
Life of Pix (http://www.lifeofpix.com/)
MMT (http://mmt.li/)
Pexels (http://www.pexels.com/)
Picography (http://picography.co/)
Pixabay (http://pixabay.com)
Raumrot (http://www.raumrot.com/)
Re:Splashed (http://www.resplashed.com/)
SplitShire (http://splitshire.com/)
Stok Pic (http://stokpic.com/)
Startup Stock Photos (http://startupstockphotos.com/)
Stock Snap (https://stocksnap.io/)
SuperFamous (http://superfamous.com/)
Wikimedia Commons (http://hyperurl.co/wikicom)
Adobe Stock (https://stock.adobe.com/)

Paid Image Options
Adobe Stock (https://stock.adobe.com/)
Dreamstime (http://dreamstime.com)
Shutterstock (http://shutterstock.com)

Fonts
1001fonts (http://1001fonts.com)
dafont (http://dafont.com)
Google Fonts (https://fonts.google.com/)

Design Software
Photoshop, Adobe Illustrator (http://adobe.com)
Gimp (http://gimp.com)

Places to Find Designers
99Designs (http://99designs.com)
Craigslist (http://craigslist.org)
Freelancer (http://freelancer.com)
Fiverr (http://fiverr.com)
T-shirt Factory (http://www.tshirt-factory.com/)
Upwork (http://upwork.com)

Reverse Image Lookup
Google Images (https://images.google.com)
TinEye (http://tineye.com)

Keyword Search
MerchantWords (http://merchantwords.com)

Pitching to the Media
Help A Reporter Out (https://www.helpareporter.com/)
Podcast Guests (http://PodcastGuests.com)

Website Resources
BigCartel.com
BigCommerce.com
GoDaddy.com
NameCheap.com
Namesilo.com
Shopify.com
SquareSpace.com
Weebly.com
Wix.com
Wordpress.org
WooCommerce.com

GeniusLink (https://www.geni.us/)

Other POD Websites
Cafepress.com
Printful (http://theprintful.com)
RedBubble.com
SpreadShirt.com
Society6.com
Zazzle.com

Books By Jill b.

Please check out my other books at **http://byjillb.com**:

The Modern Frugal American Housewife Book #1
Home Economics

The Modern Frugal American Housewife Book #2
Organic Gardening

The Modern Frugal American Housewife Book #3
Moms Edition

The Modern Frugal American Housewife Book #4
Emergency Prepping

How to Keep Backyard Chickens
A Straightforward Beginner's Guide

The Best Backyard Chicken Breeds
A List of Top Birds for Pets, Eggs and Meat

Foraging
A Beginner's Guide to Wild Edible and Medicinal Plants

Medicinal Herb Garden
10 Plants for the Self-Reliant Homestead Prepper

Hidden
Prepper's Secret Edible Garden

CAN Dos and Don'ts
Water Bath and Pressure Canning

How to Make Money on eBay: Beginner's Guide
From Setting Up Accounts to Selling Like a Pro

How to Make Money on eBay: Maximize Profits
Secrets, Stories, Tips and Hacks - Confessions of a 16-Year eBay Veteran

How to Make Money on eBay: International Sales
Taking the Fear and Guesswork Out of Doing Business Internationally on eBay

Self-Publish on a Budget with Amazon
A Guide for the Author Publishing eBooks on Kindle

How to Start a T-Shirt Business on Merch by Amazon

How To Start An Etsy Online Business
The Creative Entrepreneur's Guide

About the Author

~ Self-Reliance: One Step at a Time ~
http://byjillb.com

Reliance on one job. Reliance on the agri-industrial food system. Are you ready to break free, take control and to rely on yourself?

With a no-nonsense style, Jill Bong draws from her own homesteading experiences and mistakes, and writes books focusing on maximizing output with minimal input to save you time and money.

Jill writes under the pen name Jill b. She is an author, entrepreneur, homesteader and is the co-inventor and co-founder of Chicken Armor (http://chickenarmor.com), an affordable, low maintenance chicken saddle. She has also written over a dozen books on homesteading and self-reliance.

Jill has been mentioned/quoted in various publications including The Associated Press, The New York Times, The Denver Post and ABC News. She has written for various magazines including Countryside and Small Stock Journal, Molly Green, Farm Show Magazine and Backyard Poultry Magazine. She holds an Engineering degree from an Ivy League from a previous life.

At its height, her previous homestead included over 100 chickens, geese and ducks, as well as cats, a dog, bees and a donkey named Elvis. She currently learning permaculture techniques to apply to her homestead in rural Oregon.

Learn more by visiting her site http://byjillb.com.

Made in the USA
Columbia, SC
07 August 2022

64833738R00036